COMPONENTS OF DISCIPLESHIP

SESSION 8

INTERFACING

EVANGELISM and DISCIPLESHIP

INTERFACING

DR. AARON R. JONES
Foreword by Dr. Timothy M. Hill

Interfacing Evangelism and Discipleship

WORKBOOK

Components of Discipleship

Dr. Aaron R. Jones

Interfacing Evangelism and Discipleship – Components of Discipleship

Copyright © 2018 by Dr. Aaron R. Jones

Printed in the United States of America

Published by Kingdom Publishing, LLC, Odenton, MD 21113

All rights reserved. No part of this book may be reproduced or transmitted in any form or by any means, electronic or mechanical, including photocopying, recording or by any information storage and retrieval system without written permission from the author, except for the inclusion of brief quotations in a review.

All scripture quotations are from the King James Version of the Bible. Thomas Nelson Publishers, Nashville: Thomas Nelson, Inc. 1972

Editor: Sharon D. Jones

Graphic Designer: Janell McIlwain – JM Virtual Concepts

                Tiara Smith

ISBN 978-1-947741-23-2

Table of Contents

Interfacing Evangelism and Discipleship Sessions 1

Foreword 2

What is Christian Discipleship? 4

Characteristics of a Disciple 5

7 Conclusions to Discipleship 10

Works Cited 17

About the Author

Contact Page

Interfacing Evangelism and Discipleship
Sessions

Session 1—**Introduction and Philosophy**

Session 2—**5 Principles to Encourage Evangelism**

Session 3—**Components of Evangelism**

Session 4—**Bait for Evangelism**

Session 5—**Methodology of Evangelism**

Session 6—**Church Planting Produces Evangelism and Discipleship**

Session 7—**Babes in Christ**

Session 8—**Components of Discipleship**

Session 9—**Evangelism and Discipleship Plan**

Session 10—**Spirit of Forgiveness**

Foreword

When God calls a man of faith and fortitude to a specific purpose in the building of His Kingdom, He uses an individual like Dr. Aaron Jones.

Feeling the urgency of the hour, Dr. Jones has shaped his participation in the FINISH Commitment by emphasizing the merging of evangelism and discipleship strategies to assist churches and individuals in their quests to effectively reach the lost. As Senior Pastor of New Hope Church of God, he is well-aware of what it takes to affect the Great Commission of our Lord.

Dr. Jones' desire is to instruct others on how to deliberately make an impact on winning souls and then discipling them for powerful Christian service. His all-inclusive approach will intrigue and provide the impetus for those willing to pursue the heart of God.

Interfacing Evangelism and Discipleship will change the course of your outreach!

Dr. Timothy M. Hill
General Overseer

Foreword

Church of God, Cleveland, Tennessee

What is Christian Discipleship?

What is Christian Discipleship?

It accepts the words and workings of Jesus Christ. It involves training believers how to apply His words and workings.

___
___
___
___
___

Characteristics of a Disciple

Characteristics of a Disciple

- **D**—Desires the presence of God

___
___
___
___
___

Interfacing Evangelism and Discipleship – Components of Discipleship

- **I**—Ignites others around them by the Holy Spirit

- **S**—Stands in prayer for the church, his family, and the world

- **C**—Concerned about God's Kingdom

Characteristics of a Disciple

- **I**—Involves oneself in outreach

- **P**—Plans daily devotional time with God

- **L**—Leaves the sinful past behind

- **E**—Exemplifies the teachings of Jesus

Additional Notes

7 Conclusions to Discipleship

7 Conclusions to Discipleship[1]

Every day the world is creating disciples. The world uses things that feel good to draw disciples regardless of the consequences. The world presents a powerful influence. As believers, we are called to be followers, but not followers of this world.

_____

_____

_____

7 Conclusions to Discipleship

■ A disciple of Jesus understands that it is a command of God, a challenge from God, and a changed lifestyle for God.

■ As disciples and soldiers for Jesus Christ, we have a great assignment. Our assignment is to help others to see that the destruction of eternal lives is at stake.

Interfacing Evangelism and Discipleship – Components of Discipleship

❶ Conclusion #1— Jesus Must Be the #1 Priority

"If any man come to me, and hate not his father, and mother, and wife, and children, and brethren, and sisters, yea, and his own life also, he cannot be my disciple."

Luke 14:26

_____
_____
_____
_____
_____

❷ Conclusion #2— Must Stay on the Path (Journey)

"And whosoever doth not bear his cross, and come after me cannot be my disciple."

Luke 14:27

_____
_____
_____
_____
_____

7 Conclusions to Discipleship

❸ Conclusion #3— Must Count the Price (Cost)

"For which of you, intending to build a tower, sitteth not down first, and counteth the cost, whether he have sufficient to finish it?"

Luke 14:28

_____
_____
_____
_____
_____

❹ Conclusion #4— Must Not Cling to Earthly Possessions

"So likewise, whosoever he be of you that forsaketh not all that he hath, he cannot by my disciple."

Luke 14:33

_____
_____
_____
_____
_____

❺ Conclusion #5— Must Be Productive

"Herein is my Father glorified, that ye bear much fruit; so shall ye be my disciples."

John 15:8

_____
_____
_____
_____
_____
_____
_____

❻ Conclusion #6— Must Have Passion

"By this shall all men know that ye are my disciple, if ye have love one to another."

John 13:35

_____
_____
_____
_____
_____
_____
_____

❼ Conclusion #7— Must Know His Position

"The disciple is not above his master, nor the servant above his lord."

Matthew 10:24

_____

_____

_____

_____

_____

_____

_____

Additional Notes

Works Cited

[1]Jones, Aaron R., The Disciple's Conclusion. (Denton: Kingdom Kaught Publishing, LLC), 2015.

About the Author

DR. AARON R. JONES serves as Senior Pastor of New Hope Church of God. Under his pastorate is New Hope Kiddie Kollege, Inc (Daycare) and New Hope Community Outreach Services, Inc. Dr. Jones also oversees New Hope Church of God Ghana (2 churches) and New Hope Church of God Uganda (3 churches).

Dr. Jones is an Ordained Bishop with the Church of God denomination and is the DELMARVA-DC District Overseer (16 churches). Dr. Jones serves on DELMARVA-DC's Regional Council, Ministerial Internship Program Board, Urban Ministry Committee, Finance Committee, and Chaplain's Board. He also serves on both the Church of God's International and DELMARVA-DC Ministry to the Military Board. In his local community, Dr. Jones serves as a Chaplain for the Charles County Sheriff Department. He also serves as Board Secretary for the United Ministers Coalition of Southern Maryland, Inc.

Being obedient to 2 Timothy 2:15, "Study to show thyself approved…," Dr. Jones received a Doctorate in Theology and Pastoral Counseling from Life

Christian University and a Doctorate in Christian Counseling from American Christian College and Seminary. He is a certified Pastoral Counselor with the International Association of Christian Counseling Professionals. He is a Life and Pastoral Coach. He is the former Executive Vice President of the National Bible College and Seminary in Fort Washington, Maryland.

Dr. Jones has published ten books and a soul-wining project that provide a biblical foundation for Christian doctrine and discipline. He has recorded a CD entitled, Peace in the Storm. He is the founder and owner of God's Comfort Ministries, LLC, which provides Christian literature, evangelism training, and spiritual guidance. He has appeared live on TCT Network; WATC-TV's Atlanta Live; Babbie's House (hosted by CCM artist Babbie Mason); and In Concert Today on DCTV. He has done radio interviews with Radio One's WYCB's program; The Praise Fest Show; and online with Total Prayze. He was featured on the cover of Change Gospel Magazine and interviewed on Promoting Purpose Magazine.

Dr. Jones not only serves God, but his country as well. He has served over 20 years in the Armed Forces. He is a retired Chaplain with the Army National Guard. He participated in both Operation Noble Eagle (2003) and Operation Iraqi Freedom III (2005).

Dr. Jones is happily married to the former Sharon Russell. He sincerely believes without her love, support, and encouragement, many of his goals would not have been accomplished.

Contact Page

Mailing Address:

150 Post Office Road #1079

Waldorf, Maryland 20604

Website: www.godscomfort.net

Email: drjones@godscomfortmin.net

Facebook: God's Comfort Ministries

Twitter: @GodsComfort_Min

Instagram: @godscomfort_min

GOD'S COMFORT MINISTRIES

God's Comfort Ministries (GCM) provides practical Christian books, teachings, trainings, and coaching to new converts and seasoned believers. GCM provides understanding of the doctrinal principles of the Bible.

Services Provided

Pastoral and Life Coaching

Evangelism and Discipleship Training

Spiritual Guidance

New Author Consultation

Christian Literature